JUNIOR BIOS

Michelle Obama

BY HAYLEY NORRIS

Enslow PUBLISHING

Please visit our website, www.enslow.com. For a free color catalog of all our high-quality books, call toll free 1-800-398-2504 or fax 1-877-980-4454.

Library of Congress Cataloging-in-Publication Data

Names: Norris, Hayley, author.
Title: Michelle Obama / Hayley Norris.
Description: New York : Enslow Publishing, [2021] | Series: Junior bios | Includes bibliographical references and index. | Contents: From Chicago to D.C. – A stellar student – College years– Giving back – Off to the White House – After the White House – Inspiring others – Michelle through time.
Identifiers: LCCN 2019060009 | ISBN 9781978518995 ; (library binding) | ISBN 9781978518971 ; (paperback) | ISBN 9781978518988 ; (6 Pack) | ISBN 9781978519008 ; (ebook)
Subjects: LCSH: Obama, Michelle, 1964--Juvenile literature. | Presidents' spouses--United States--Biography--Juvenile literature. | Political activists--United States--Biography--Juvenile literature. | Women philanthropists--United States--Biography--Juvenile literature.
Classification: LCC E909.O24 N667 2020 | DDC 973.932092 [B]--dc23
LC record available at https://lccn.loc.gov/2019060009

Published in 2021 by
Enslow Publishing
101 West 23rd Street, Suite #240
New York, NY 10011

Designer: Sarah Liddell
Editor: Kate Mikoley

Photo credits: Cover, p. 1 (Michelle Obama) EPG_EuroPhotoGraphics/Shutterstock.com; cover, p. 1 (photo frame) Aleksandr Andrushkiv/Shutterstock.com; marble texture used throughout HardtIllustrations/Shutterstock.com; lined paper texture used throughout Mtsaride/Shutterstock.com; watercolor texture used throughout solarbird/Shutterstock.com; pp. 5, 7 Pool/Pool/Getty Images News/Getty Images; p. 8 David Paul Morris/Stringer/Getty Images News/Getty Images; p. 11 Brooks Kraft/Contributor/Corbis News/Getty Images; pp. 13, 15 Alex Wong/Staff/Getty Images News/Getty Images; p. 16 Mike Coppola/Staff/Getty Images Entertainment/Getty Images; p. 19 Drew Angerer/Staff/Getty Images News/Getty Images.

Portions of this work were originally authored by Sarah Machajewski and published as *Michelle Obama*. All new material this edition authored by Hayley Norris.

Printed in the United States of America

Some of the images in this book illustrate individuals who are models. The depictions do not imply actual situations or events.

CPSIA compliance information: Batch #BS20ENS: For further information contact Enslow Publishing, New York, New York, at 1-800-542-2595.

Contents

Words in the glossary appear in **bold** type the first time they are used in the text.

From Chicago to DC

Michelle Obama has been a public figure since 2007, when her husband, Barack Obama, announced he was running for president. When Barack took office in 2009, Michelle became First Lady—a postion that put her even more in the spotlight. During the eight years the Obamas lived in the White House, Michelle used this position to bring awareness to causes she cared about and help others.

Before everyone knew her name, Michelle was a kid growing up in Chicago, Illinois. She worked hard and took pride in doing well in school. Her **work ethic** helped her become the woman she is today.

BARACK OBAMA WAS THE FIRST AFRICAN AMERICAN TO BE PRESIDENT OF THE UNITED STATES. MICHELLE WAS THE FIRST AFRICAN AMERICAN TO BE FIRST LADY.

A Stellar Student

Before she was Michelle Obama, she was Michelle LaVaughn Robinson. Born on January 17, 1964, in Chicago, Michelle grew up in a small apartment on the city's South Side. Her father, Fraser, worked for the Chicago Water Department. Her mother, Marian, was a stay-at-home mom, raising Michelle and her older brother, Craig.

In Her Own Words

*"One of the lessons that I grew up with was to always stay true to yourself and never let what somebody else says **distract** you from your goals."*

MICHELLE'S MOTHER MOVED INTO THE WHITE HOUSE AFTER BARACK OBAMA BECAME PRESIDENT. SHE HELPED CARE FOR MICHELLE AND BARACK'S DAUGHTERS, SASHA AND MALIA.

Fraser and Marian Robinson worked hard and taught their children to do so too. Michelle and her brother both learned to read at an early age. Michelle attended Chicago public schools and was an excellent student. She did so well in elementary school that she skipped second grade.

MICHELLE WAS THE SALUTATORIAN, OR STUDENT WITH THE SECOND-HIGHEST GRADES, OF HER HIGH SCHOOL CLASS. NOW, SHE SPEAKS TO STUDENTS AT SCHOOLS AROUND THE WORLD.

When Michelle was in sixth grade, she was chosen to be part of a program that let her learn French and take advanced science classes in school.

For high school, Michelle attended Chicago's first magnet school, Whitney M. Young Magnet High School. Magnet schools are public schools that offer special programs and classes. Michelle's high school focused on preparing students for college. She took advanced classes and joined the National Honor Society, a group that recognizes high school students based on academic accomplishments, leadership, service, and character. She was also the **treasurer** of the student council, or government.

In Her Own Words

"I want our young people to know that they matter, that they belong ... Don't be afraid ... Be **determined**. Be hopeful. Be **empowered**. Empower yourselves with a good education, then get out there and use that education to build a country worthy of your boundless promise."

College Years

After high school, Michelle went to one of the top colleges in the country, Princeton University. The hard-working spirit Michelle grew up with followed her to Princeton. She studied **sociology** and African American studies. In 1985, Michelle graduated from Princeton with honors.

FACTS BEHIND THE FIGURE

During law school, Michelle worked at the Harvard Legal Aid Bureau. This organization helps people in **marginalized** communities who don't have a lot of money by providing free legal services. Law students help people with government benefits, housing questions, and other matters.

MICHELLE GRADUATED FROM HARVARD LAW SCHOOL IN 1988.

During Michelle's time at Princeton, the school was quite socially segregated. This meant the small number of black students didn't often mix with white students. Michelle wrote her **thesis** on the experience of being black in a mostly white school.

After Princeton, Michelle went on to study law at Harvard University. She was interested in how lawyers could help people.

Giving Back

After law school, Michelle became a lawyer for Sidley & Austin, a law firm in Chicago. There, she met Barack Obama, who she would later marry.

FACTS BEHIND THE FIGURE

Volunteering is an important part of Michelle's life. During Barack's presidency, she and her family volunteered at homeless shelters and soup kitchens around Washington, DC. After leaving the White House, she's continued to give back and encourages others to do the same.

MICHELLE OFTEN SPEAKS AT SCHOOLS, TALKING TO STUDENTS ABOUT THE IMPORTANCE OF VOLUNTEERING, OR HELPING OTHERS WITHOUT HAVING TO.

Soon, Michelle realized her true calling was to help people and give back to her community. Michelle took a job with the City of Chicago. Later, she became the director of the Chicago chapter of Public Allies, a group that gets young people ready for jobs in public service.

In 1996, Michelle started working at the University of Chicago. While serving as the **associate dean** of student services, she created a community service program and helped students get involved with volunteering.

Off to the White House

Barack was elected as an Illinois state senator in 1996. In 2004, he was elected to the U.S. Senate. During this time, the Obamas were also raising two daughters, Malia and Sasha. Both parents worked while raising their children.

FACTS BEHIND THE FIGURE

In 2008, Barack Obama was elected president of the United States. He was elected again in 2012. As First Lady, Michelle started Let's Move! in 2010, aiming to make ideas about healthy living available to everyone. It encouraged kids to find exercises they enjoy, and worked to provide healthier food to children around the country.

MICHELLE PLANTED A GARDEN AT THE WHITE HOUSE IN 2009. KIDS OFTEN VISITED TO HELP WITH IT. SHE ENCOURAGED PEOPLE AROUND THE COUNTRY TO GROW THEIR OWN FRESH VEGETABLES.

In 2007, Barack announced he was running for president, and the Obama family quickly became famous. Michelle played a big role in her husband's campaign. She traveled, made speeches, and met with people around the country to gain their support. However, Michelle still focused on her family first. She's said her most important job is to be a good mother to her daughters.

COLLEGE SIGNING DAY STILL HAPPENS TODAY. MICHELLE SPEAKS AT EVENTS CELEBRATING STUDENTS' ACCOMPLISHMENTS AND URGING THEM TO KEEP LEARNING.

In 2011, along with Dr. Jill Biden, Michelle started Joining Forces. This **initiative** encouraged Americans to support military members, people who have served in the military, and military families by offering programs in education, health care, and employment.

Another initiative, called Reach Higher, encouraged students to continue their education after high school through professional training programs, community colleges, and four-year colleges. Each year since 2015, Michelle has invited students who have committed to going to college to celebrate College Signing Day. Students around the country wear clothing with their decided college's name on it, take pictures, and share them online using the hashtag #ReachHigher.

FACTS BEHIND THE FIGURE

In 2015, Michelle helped to start Let Girls Learn, a U.S. government initiative that helped girls all over the world attend and stay in school.

After the White House

Barack Obama served two terms as president and left office in 2017. Michelle may not live in the White House anymore, but that hasn't stopped her from working hard or fighting for causes she believes in.

FACTS BEHIND THE FIGURE

In 2018, Michelle came out with an **autobiography** called *Becoming*. The book quickly became a best seller. In it, Michelle wrote about experiences that made her who she is today—from her childhood in Chicago to life in the White House.

IN HER BOOK BECOMING, MICHELLE ALSO WROTE ABOUT MOTHERHOOD AND HER MARRIAGE.

Michelle and Barack both work closely with their **nonprofit** group, the Obama Foundation. One of the foundation's programs, the Girls Opportunity Alliance, is especially important to Michelle. In many parts of the world, girls don't have the same learning opportunities that boys do. The Girls Opportunity Alliance aims to empower young girls all over the world through education. It helps community leaders, raises money, and inspires people to get involved with the cause.

Inspiring Others

Michelle's commitment to helping others has made her a role model to people around the world. As a law student, she worked to help people in underserved communities. As First Lady, she helped raise awareness about healthy habits, brought understanding to the challenges faced by people in the military, and inspired young people to continue their educations.

Even after her time in the White House, Michelle Obama still helps others and speaks out for causes she cares about. Through her actions and her writing, she's sure to inspire people for years to come.

Michelle's Timeline

1964: MICHELLE IS BORN ON JANUARY 17, IN CHICAGO, ILLINOIS.

1985: MICHELLE GRADUATES PRINCETON UNIVERSITY.

1988: MICHELLE GRADUATES FROM HARVARD LAW SCHOOL. SHE BEGINS WORKING AT THE CHICAGO LAW FIRM SIDLEY & AUSTIN.

1992: MICHELLE MARRIES BARACK OBAMA.

2009: BARACK TAKES OFFICE AS PRESIDENT OF THE UNITED STATES. MICHELLE BECOMES THE FIRST AFRICAN AMERICAN FIRST LADY.

2010: MICHELLE LAUNCHES LET'S MOVE!

2011: MICHELLE LAUNCHES JOINING FORCES WITH DR. JILL BIDEN.

2012: BARACK WINS A SECOND TERM AS PRESIDENT, MAKING MICHELLE THE FIRST LADY FOR ANOTHER FOUR YEARS.

2014: MICHELLE LAUNCHES REACH HIGHER.

2015: MICHELLE FIRST INVITES STUDENTS TO TAKE PART IN COLLEGE SIGNING DAY.

MICHELLE LAUNCHES LET GIRLS LEARN.

2018: MICHELLE RELEASES *BECOMING*.

Glossary

associate dean The head of a school or division at a university or college.

autobiography A book written by someone about their life.

determined Deciding that you are going to do something and not let anyone or anything stop you.

distract To take someone's attention away.

empowered Having the means, confidence, knowledge, or ability to do things for oneself.

initiative An act or strategy to improve a situation.

marginalized Put in a powerless or unimportant position in a society.

nonprofit An organization that is not run for the sake of making a profit.

sociology The study of societies and relationships between people.

thesis A long essay involving research that is written to earn a college degree.

treasurer The person in charge of the money that is taken in and paid out by a group.

work ethic A set of values based on the importance of hard work.

For More Information

Books

Cooke, Tim. *Michelle Obama*. New York, NY: Gareth Stevens Publishing, 2020.

Leaf, Christina. *Michelle Obama: Health Advocate*. Minneapolis, MN: Bellwether Media, 2019.

Wilson, Lakita. *Michelle Obama: Get to Know the Influential First Lady and Education Advocate*. North Mankato, MN: Capstone Press, 2020.

Websites

Michelle Obama
www.whitehouse.gov/about-the-white-house/first-ladies/michelle-obama/
Find out more about Michelle on the official White House website.

Obama Foundation
www.obama.org/
Learn more about Michelle and Barack's work with the Obama Foundation here.

Publisher's note to educators and parents: Our editors have carefully reviewed these websites to ensure that they are suitable for students. Many websites change frequently, however, and we cannot guarantee that a site's future contents will continue to meet our high standards of quality and educational value. Be advised that students should be closely supervised whenever they access the internet.

Index